Best Wishes

....

....

....

....

....

....

....

....

....

....

....

....

....

....

**May the future
bring...**

This Book Belongs to:

....

....

Graduating from:

....

....

....

Date:

....

Graduation Journal

Written and Illustrated by

Lynn Phang

**Andrews McMeel
Publishing**

Kansas City

Graduation Journal

For information, write Andrews McMeel Publishing, an Andrews McMeel Universal company, 4520 Main Street, Kansas City, Missouri 64111

01 02 03 04 05 TWP 9 8 7 6 5 4 3 2 1

ISBN: 0-7407-0763-9

Library of Congress Catalog Card Number: 00-106900

♥

To Sarah & Andrea
for their help
and recent rite of passage
&
Mindy for making this
so much fun

ALL ABOUT ME!

My Birthday

....

I was born on a:

_____ a. Sunny day

_____ b. Rainy day

_____ c. *Early!* in the season

_____ d. Other _____

In:

_____ a. A small, sleepy town

_____ b. A big, bustling city

_____ c. I wasn't born; I was hatched

_____ d. Other _____

ALL ABOUT ME!

Interesting Facts About My Birth!

The Perfect Time

In the wee hours at _____A.M.

(I was always a night owl) at _____P.M.

My Weight

A lean, mean, fighting machine _____ lbs.

An average but unique _____ lbs.

A heavyweight champion _____ lbs.

Other Unknown Facts

....

....

....

....

....

ALL ABOUT ME!

This Is Me When I Was Born!

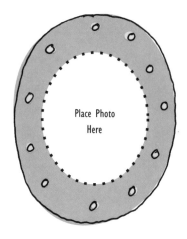

Place Photo Here

_____ a. A quiet, sleepy baby

_____ b. A noisy, active baby

_____ c. A hungry baby

_____ d. Other _____

The First Thing My Parents Noticed About Me

....

....

....

....

ALL ABOUT ME!

This Is Me Now!

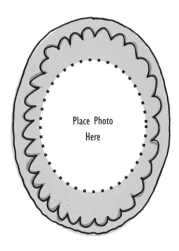

Place Photo Here

_____	a.	Quiet and introspective
_____	b.	Outgoing and friendly
_____	c.	Food is good!
_____	d.	Other _____

Some Things Haven't Changed!

....

....

....

....

ALL ABOUT ME!

Me and My Favorite Toy

Toy Name: _____

I called my toy: _____

I got my favorite toy:

_____ a. As a birthday gift

_____ b. As a holiday gift

_____ c. Because I *begged* and whined for it!

_____ d. Other _____

More Stuff About My Favorite Toy!

(e.g., "I took my toy everywhere" or "I slept with my toy *every* night.")

....

....

....

ALL ABOUT ME!

My Favorite Childhood Picture

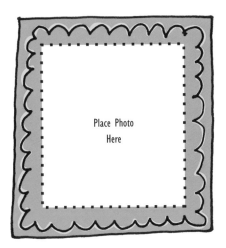

Place Photo
Here

I love this picture because (check all that apply):

_____ a. I'm so cute!

_____ b. It's all in the attitude!

_____ c. That smile, those eyes!

_____ d. Other _____

....

....

....

ALL ABOUT ME!

My birthday makes me a bona fide:

_____ Aquarius (Jan. 20 – Feb. 18)

_____ Pisces (Feb. 19 – March 20)

_____ Aries (March 21 – April 19)

_____ Taurus (April 20 – May 20)

_____ Gemini (May 21 – June 21)

_____ Cancer (June 22 – July 22)

_____ Leo (July 23 – Aug. 22)

_____ Virgo (Aug. 23 – Sept. 22)

_____ Libra (Sept. 23 – Oct. 23)

_____ Scorpio (Oct. 24 – Nov. 21)

_____ Sagittarius (Nov. 22 – Dec. 21)

_____ Capricorn (Dec. 22 – Jan. 19)

_____ I was born on the cusp, baby!

ALL ABOUT ME!

What They Say About My Sign   What They Say About ME!

Personality

☺

....

....

....

Love Life

♡

....

....

....

Future

⭐

....

Other

?

....

ALL ABOUT ME!

My Favorite Stuff

....

....

....

Favorite Colors

.... the color of (the) ....

.... which reminds me of ....

.... the color of my favorite ....

Other (Be creative! For example, the color of dreams.)

....

....

....

ALL ABOUT ME!

Favorite Car

Make: _____

Year: _____

Color: _____

_____ a. Speeding on the coast, in the south of France
_____ b. Packed full with my friends going to a party
_____ c. My favorite of my large collection of cars
_____ d. Other _____

My Current Mode of Transport

_____ a. I've got two feet
_____ b. Please Mom/Dad/Sister/Brother!
_____ c. I've got wheels! _____
_____ d. Other _____

No one knows about the time I borrowed the car and . . .

....

....

ALL ABOUT ME!

My Favorite Snack

....

Best eaten:

_____ a. In front of the TV

_____ b. While doing homework

_____ c. Whenever possible

_____ d. Other _____

My Favorite Food

....

_____ a. Healthy but delicious

_____ b. Salty and savory

_____ c. Sweet like *moi!*

_____ d. Other _____

ALL ABOUT ME!

My Favorite Store(s)

In the mall: _____

On the Web: _____

Catalog: _____

Other: _____

The *best* deal:

....

....

My shameful splurge:

....

....

I can't believe I wanted . . .

....

ALL ABOUT ME!

My Favorite Web Site(s)

For great deals visit:

www._____   www._____
www._____   www._____

For celebrity dish visit:

www._____   www._____
www._____   www._____

For the best chat rooms visit:

www._____   www._____

For _____ visit:

www._____   www._____
www._____   www._____

....

ALL ABOUT ME!

My Favorite Books(s)

_____ by _____
made me laugh until I cried.

_____ by _____
just made me cry!

_____ by _____
made me double-check under my bed before I go to sleep!

_____ by _____
is _____.

My Favorite Magazines

....

....

....

....

HIGH SCHOOL

The High School(s) I Attended

.... at ....

.... at ....

Our Mascot

....

HIGH SCHOOL

I was a freshman

in the year of _____.

A year that will be remembered for:

_____ a. Scandalous politics
_____ b. The year I got braces
_____ c. The year I was a freshman
_____ d. Other _____

More on My Freshman Year

....

....

....

....

....

....

....

HIGH SCHOOL

High school was:

_____ a. A great experience

_____ b. Fun — but what's next?

_____ c. Boring

_____ d. Other _____

One thing I would seriously consider changing about high school:

_____ a. The location

_____ b. The general concept of high school

_____ c. My hair

_____ d. Other _____

More Notes (No Pun Intended)

....

....

....

....

HIGH SCHOOL

The Best Thing About High School

_____ a. The teachers and the classes
_____ b. My friends
_____ c. Hello — it is my stepping stone to world fame!
_____ d. Other _____

....

....

The Worst Thing About High School

_____ a. The teachers and the classes
_____ b. _Some_ people
_____ c. Getting in my way to world fame!
_____ d. Other _____

....

....

....

HIGH SCHOOL

My Favorite Class

....

This was my favorite class because:

_____ a. This was (and still is) my *best* subject!

_____ b. It gave me an idea of what I want to do next!

_____ c. It was challenging but fun.

_____ d. Other _____

My Greatest Accomplishment in Class

....

....

....

....

....

....

....

HIGH SCHOOL

My Favorite Teacher

....

He/She was my favorite teacher because:

_____ a. Of the cool subject!_____

_____ b. He/She was a great teacher and a great friend.

_____ c. He/She was *tough* but fair.

_____ d. Other _____

A Funny Moment in My Favorite Teacher's Class

....

....

....

....

....

....

....

SCHOOL TEAMS
& Activities

SPORTS

My Favorite Sports

_____ Football	_____ Tennis	_____ Field Hockey
_____ Soccer	_____ Track	_____ Volleyball
_____ Swimming	_____ Gymnastics	_____ Baseball

_____ Other _____

The Teams That I Was On!

_____ Football	_____ Tennis	_____ Field Hockey
_____ Soccer	_____ Track	_____ Volleyball
_____ Swimming	_____ Gymnastics	_____ Baseball

_____ Other _____

SCHOOL TEAMS
& Activities

Our Proudest Moment

....

....

....

....

....

....

The Team Members I Will Never Forget

....

....

....

....

....

....

SCHOOL TEAMS
& Activities

My Other Activities

_____ Drama	_____ Jazz Band	_____ Chess
_____ Concert Band	_____ Choir	_____ Reading Club
_____ Marching Band	_____ Cheerleading	_____ Other (list below)

Our Proudest Moment

....

....

....

....

....

....

....

Place Photo

Here

Us at Play!

SCHOOL TEAMS
& Activities

A HILARIOUS Moment with the Team

....

....

....

....

....

....

....

....

....

....

....

....

SCHOOL TEAMS
& Activities

The Greatest Lesson I Learned from My Teammates

....

....

....

....

....

....

....

....

....

....

....

....

Hobbies

My favorite "after-school" hobby:

_____ a. Music

_____ b. Arts and crafts

_____ c. Being a couch potato

_____ d. Other _____

I love my hobby because (check all that apply):

_____ a. Totally fun!

_____ b. I'm great at it!

_____ c. It makes someone happy.

_____ d. Other _____

Hobbies

More on My Hobby!

....

....

....

....

....

....

....

....

....

....

Confession Corner

My Most Embarrassing Moment!

....

....

....

....

....

....

....

....

....

....

....

....

....

....

Confession Corner

The Rating

😣 _____ I will never live it down.

😵 _____ It will be funny in ten years.

😖 _____ It will be funny in five years.

😐 _____ Will the ground please swallow me up.

🙂 _____ I am over it already.

One More Thing No One Knows!

....

....

....

....

....

....

....

GOSSIP CENTRAL

The Juiciest Story This Year

....

....

....

....

....

....

....

....

....

....

....

....

....

GOSSIP CENTRAL

Rating

_____
_____
_____
_____
_____

My Attitude Toward Gossip

_____ a. A necessary evil.

_____ b. If you don't have something nice to say, come
sit next to me.

_____ c. Fun only if harmless.

_____ d. Other _____

....

....

....

My Proudest Moment

My proudest moment was made extraspecial by:

_____ a. My family's support

_____ b. Knowing I helped someone

_____ c. Knowing I achieved something I worked hard for

_____ d. Other _____

....

....

....

....

....

....

....

....

....

....

....

....

In/Out – Fashion

....

....

....   Nail Polish

....

....   Lipstick
                                                          & Make-up
....

....   JEANS
                                                           Brands
....   & Styles

....

....   SHOES
                                                           Brands
....   & Styles

....

....

....

....

....

....

....

....

....

....

Fashion Collage

Place Photos of

Your Favorite Models,

Designers, Designer Clothing, etc.,

Here

Me Looking My Best!

My favorite everyday outfit to wear consisted of:

_____ a. Jeans and a tiny T

_____ b. _____ and a *mini* skirt

_____ c. Sweats

_____ d. Who cares!

Me Looking My Best!

My Style

_____	a.	Cool & Funky
_____	b.	Glam & Fab
_____	c.	Down to Earth
_____	d.	What's Style?

My Favorite Jeans

Brand: _____

Color: _____

Style: _____

My Favorite Shirt

Brand: _____

Color: _____

Style: _____

My Favorite Shoes

Brand: _____

Color: _____

Style: _____

My Favorite Dress

Brand: _____

Color: _____

Style: _____

More FAVE Stuff

....

....

TV – My Picks

Best Comedy

....

Leading Actor

....

Leading Actress

....

Supporting Actor

....

Supporting Actress

....

Best Drama

....

Leading Actor

....

Leading Actress

....

Supporting Actor

....

Supporting Actress

....

TV – My Picks

Best Miniseries

....

Leading Actor

....

Leading Actress

....

Supporting Actor

....

Supporting Actress

....

Best Made-for-TV Movie

....

Leading Actor

....

Leading Actress

....

Supporting Actor

....

Supporting Actress

....

TV Collage

Place Photos of

Your Favorite TV

Actors, Actresses, etc.,

Here

SOAPS – My Picks

Best Soap Opera

....

Leading Actor

....

Leading Actress

....

Supporting Actor

....

Supporting Actress

....

The BEST Episode
and What I Would Have Done

....

....

....

....

....

MUSIC – My Picks

Pop/Rock

Female Artist

....

Male Artist

....

Band

....

CD

....

Soul/Rhythm & Blues

Female Artist

....

Male Artist

....

Band

....

CD

....

MUSIC – My Picks

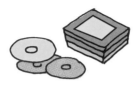

Rap/Hip-Hop

Female Artist

....

Male Artist

....

Band

....

CD

....

Country

Female Artist

....

Male Artist

....

Band

....

CD

....

MUSIC – My Picks

Latin

Female Artist

....

Male Artist

....

Band

....

CD

....

Alternative

Female Artist

....

Male Artist

....

Band

....

CD

....

MUSIC – My Picks

My favorite CD makes me feel:

_____ a. Like dancing

_____ b. Like thinking and relaxing

_____ c. Like falling asleep

_____ d. Other _____

....

....

....

....

....

....

....

....

....

Movies – My Picks

Favorite Movie

....

Favorite Actor

....

Favorite Actress

....

Favorite Music Score

....

Favorite Special Effects

....

Favorite _____

....

Movies – My Picks

Favorite Action Film

....

Favorite Sci-Fi Film

....

Favorite Tearjerker

....

Favorite Comedy

....

Favorite _____

....

Videos/DVDs

I've watched _____ on
video/DVD _____ times and here's why!

....

....

....

....

....

....

....

....

....

....

....

....

Tinsel Town's Hottest Babes!

Sexiest

....

Cutest

....

Most Romantic

....

Most Dateable

....

My Best Bud

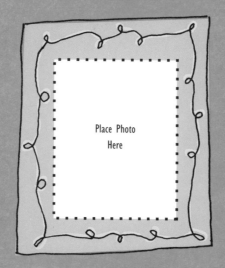

Place Photo
Here

Name

....

Birthday

....

Sign

....

My Best Bud

(Ask your best bud to fill this in, or fill it in yourself)

Favorite Food: _____

Favorite Color: _____

Favorite School Activity: _____

Favorite _____: _____

Big Crush: _____

BIG DREAM

....

....

....

....

....

....

My Best Bud

Best Personality Trait

(Check all that apply!)

_____ a. Great listener and gives great advice

_____ b. Makes me laugh

_____ c. Really fun to be with

_____ d. Other _____

Why My Best Bud Is Like No Other!

....

....

....

....

....

....

....

....

My Best Bud

Place Photos of Your Best Bud and

Your Best Bud's Favorite Things, etc.,

Here

My Gang

Without these guys, high school wouldn't have been as:

_____ a. Fun

_____ b. Eventful

_____ c. Interesting

_____ d. Other _____

Names

....

....

....

....

....

....

....

....

....

....

Things We Did

Our Best Idea

....

....

....

Our Worst Idea

....

....

....

Our _____ Idea

....

....

....

BEST BUDS ON THE RAMPAGE

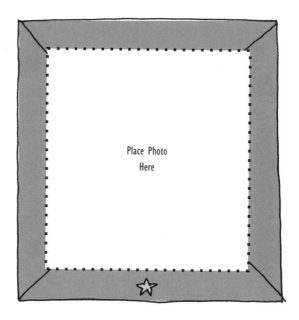

Place Photo Here

Us Together!

Date:

....

BEST BUDS ON THE RAMPAGE

*Our Most*_____*Time Together!*

_____ a. Hilarious
_____ b. Embarrassing
_____ c. Favorite
_____ d. Other _____

....

....

....

....

....

....

....

....

....

....

GUYS

Name

....

_____ a.   My main squeeze

_____ b.   My secret crush

_____ c.   The high school hunk

_____ d.   My pet (Who needs guys anyway?)

_____ e.   Other

_____

_____

_____

GUYS

How We Met

....

....

....

....

....

Our Favorite Thing to Do Together

....

....

....

....

GUYS

His Favorite Things to Do

HIS BIG DREAM

GUYS

Place Photos of You and Your Fave Guy, etc.,

Here

HOW I WILL CHANGE THE WORLD

I will change the world by:

_____ a. Helping others

_____ b. Curing _____ for mankind

_____ c. Being internationally famous

_____ d. Other _____

....

....

....

....

....

....

....

....

....

....

....

....

ONE YEAR from NOW

Where I Will Be in One Year

_____ a. In college

_____ b. Traveling in _____

_____ c. Looking at the stars

_____ d. Other _____

My Wildest Dream

....

....

....

....

....

....

....

....

....

....

FIVE YEARS
from
NOW

Where I Will Be in Five Years

_____ a. Running an international corporation

_____ b. Married with _____ children

_____ c. Looking at the stars

_____ d. Other _____

My Wildest Dream

....

....

....

....

....

....

....

....

....

....

TEN YEARS from NOW

Where I Will Be in Ten Years

_____ a. Retired, having sold my international corporation

_____ b. Relaxing on the beach of my private island

_____ c. Looking at the stars

_____ d. Other _____

My Wildest Dream

....

....

....

....

....

....

....

MY HOME, MY CASTLE

My current room:

_____ a   Reflects the chaos of my inner soul
_____ b.   Is my haven of retreat
_____ c.   Needs to be vacuumed
_____ d.   Other   _____

My Favorite Stuff
(list your favorite posters, pictures, etc.)

....

....

....

....

....

....

....

....

MY HOME, MY CASTLE

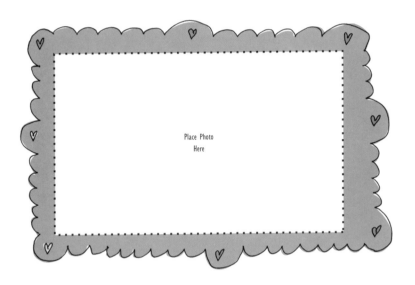

Place Photo
Here

Prom

Date

....

Theme

....

Location

....

Place Photo

Here

Prom

Corsage

....

The Restaurant We Went To

....

Who We Went With

....

....

....

....

....

Prom

The _____thing that happened!

_____ a   Most romantic

_____ b. Most unexpected

_____ c. Funniest

_____ d. Other _____

....

....

....

....

....

....

....

....

....

Prom

Overall Date Rating

_____ a   Dream boat

_____ b.   Crush come true

_____ c.   Disaster date

_____ d.   Other _____

....

....

....

....

....

....

....

....

....

Prom

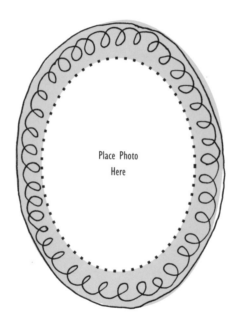

Place Photo
Here

The Prom King and Queen

....

My Choice of Prom King and Queen

....

Prom

GRADUATION

GRADUATION

Date

....

Location

....

GRADUATION

My Achievements and Awards

(Don't forget to include your high school diploma!)

....

....

....

....

....

....

....

....

....

....

....

Place Photo

Here

Place Photo

Here

GRADUATION

Who Attended with Me!

Family

....

....

....

Relatives

....

....

....

Friends

....

....

....

What I Will Never Forget

_____ a. Hard work pays off!

_____ b. Friends and family are all you need.

_____ c. The only way now is up!

_____ d. Other _____

....

....

....

....

....

....

....

....

....

....

....

....

....

....

What I Will Never Forget

....

....

....

....

....

....

....

....

....

....

....

....

....

CONTACT INFO
A – B

Name ....

Most Likely to ....

Address ....

....

Phone ....

Cell/Pager ....

E-mail ....

College/Other ....

Name ....

Most Likely to ....

Address ....

....

Phone ....

Cell/Pager ....

E-mail ....

College/Other ....

Name ....

Most Likely to ....

Address ....

....

Phone ....

Cell/Pager ....

E-mail ....

College/Other ....

Name ....

Most Likely to ....

Address ....

....

Phone ....

Cell/Pager ....

E-mail ....

College/Other ....

CONTACT INFO
C – D

Name ....

Most Likely to ....

Address ....

....

Phone ....

Cell/Pager ....

E-mail ....

College/Other ....

Name ....

Most Likely to ....

Address ....

....

Phone ....

Cell/Pager ....

E-mail ....

College/Other ....

Name ....

Most Likely to ....

Address ....

....

Phone ....

Cell/Pager ....

E-mail ....

College/Other ....

Name ....

Most Likely to ....

Address ....

....

Phone ....

Cell/Pager ....

E-mail ....

College/Other ....

CONTACT INFO
E – F

Name ....

Most Likely to ....

Address ....

....

Phone ....

Cell/Pager ....

E-mail ....

College/Other ....

Name ....

Most Likely to ....

Address ....

....

Phone ....

Cell/Pager ....

E-mail ....

College/Other ....

Name ....

Most Likely to ....

Address ....

....

Phone ....

Cell/Pager ....

E-mail ....

College/Other ....

Name ....

Most Likely to ....

Address ....

....

Phone ....

Cell/Pager ....

E-mail ....

College/Other ....

CONTACT INFO
G – H

Name ....
Most Likely to ....
Address ....
....
Phone ....
Cell/Pager ....
E-mail ....
College/Other ....

Name ....
Most Likely to ....
Address ....
....
Phone ....
Cell/Pager ....
E-mail ....
College/Other ....

Name ....
Most Likely to ....
Address ....
....
Phone ....
Cell/Pager ....
E-mail ....
College/Other ....

Name ....
Most Likely to ....
Address ....
....
Phone ....
Cell/Pager ....
E-mail ....
College/Other ....

CONTACT INFO
I – J

Name ....

Most Likely to ....

Address ....

....

Phone ....

Cell/Pager ....

E-mail ....

College/Other ....

Name ....

Most Likely to ....

Address ....

....

Phone ....

Cell/Pager ....

E-mail ....

College/Other ....

Name ....

Most Likely to ....

Address ....

....

Phone ....

Cell/Pager ....

E-mail ....

College/Other ....

Name ....

Most Likely to ....

Address ....

....

Phone ....

Cell/Pager ....

E-mail ....

College/Other ....

CONTACT INFO
K – L

Name ....

Most Likely to ....

Address ....

....

Phone ....

Cell/Pager ....

E-mail ....

College/Other ....

Name ....

Most Likely to ....

Address ....

....

Phone ....

Cell/Pager ....

E-mail ....

College/Other ....

Name ....

Most Likely to ....

Address ....

....

Phone ....

Cell/Pager ....

E-mail ....

College/Other ....

Name ....

Most Likely to ....

Address ....

....

Phone ....

Cell/Pager ....

E-mail ....

College/Other ....

CONTACT INFO
M – N

Name ....

Most Likely to ....

Address ....

....

Phone ....

Cell/Pager ....

E-mail ....

College/Other ....

Name ....

Most Likely to ....

Address ....

....

Phone ....

Cell/Pager ....

E-mail ....

College/Other ....

Name ....

Most Likely to ....

Address ....

....

Phone ....

Cell/Pager ....

E-mail ....

College/Other ....

Name ....

Most Likely to ....

Address ....

....

Phone ....

Cell/Pager ....

E-mail ....

College/Other ....

CONTACT INFO
O – P

Name ....

Most Likely to ....

Address ....

....

Phone ....

Cell/Pager ....

E-mail ....

College/Other ....

Name ....

Most Likely to ....

Address ....

....

Phone ....

Cell/Pager ....

E-mail ....

College/Other ....

Name ....

Most Likely to ....

Address ....

....

Phone ....

Cell/Pager ....

E-mail ....

College/Other ....

Name ....

Most Likely to ....

Address ....

....

Phone ....

Cell/Pager ....

E-mail ....

College/Other ....

CONTACT INFO
Q – R

Name ....

Most Likely to ....

Address ....

....

Phone ....

Cell/Pager ....

E-mail ....

College/Other ....

Name ....

Most Likely to ....

Address ....

....

Phone ....

Cell/Pager ....

E-mail ....

College/Other ....

Name ....

Most Likely to ....

Address ....

....

Phone ....

Cell/Pager ....

E-mail ....

College/Other ....

Name ....

Most Likely to ....

Address ....

....

Phone ....

Cell/Pager ....

E-mail ....

College/Other ....

CONTACT INFO
S – T

Name ....

Most Likely to ....

Address ....

....

Phone ....

Cell/Pager ....

E-mail ....

College/Other ....

Name ....

Most Likely to ....

Address ....

....

Phone ....

Cell/Pager ....

E-mail ....

College/Other ....

Name ....

Most Likely to ....

Address ....

....

Phone ....

Cell/Pager ....

E-mail ....

College/Other ....

Name ....

Most Likely to ....

Address ....

....

Phone ....

Cell/Pager ....

E-mail ....

College/Other ....

CONTACT INFO
U – V – W

Name ....

Most Likely to ....

Address ....

....

Phone ....

Cell/Pager ....

E-mail ....

College/Other ....

Name ....

Most Likely to ....

Address ....

....

Phone ....

Cell/Pager ....

E-mail ....

College/Other ....

Name ....

Most Likely to ....

Address ....

....

Phone ....

Cell/Pager ....

E-mail ....

College/Other ....

Name ....

Most Likely to ....

Address ....

....

Phone ....

Cell/Pager ....

E-mail ....

College/Other ....

CONTACT INFO
X – Y – Z

Name ....

Most Likely to ....

Address ....

....

Phone ....

Cell/Pager ....

E-mail ....

College/Other ....

Name ....

Most Likely to ....

Address ....

....

Phone ....

Cell/Pager ....

E-mail ....

College/Other ....

Name ....

Most Likely to ....

Address ....

....

Phone ....

Cell/Pager ....

E-mail ....

College/Other ....

Name ....

Most Likely to ....

Address ....

....

Phone ....

Cell/Pager ....

E-mail ....

College/Other ....

NOTES

....

....

....

....

....

....

....

....

....

....

....

....

....

....

NOTES

....

....

....

....

....

....

....

....

....

....

....

....

....

....

AUTOGRAPHS

AUTOGRAPHS

AUTOGRAPHS

AUTOGRAPHS

AUTOGRAPHS